RONALD RIDOUT
Your English
4

Longman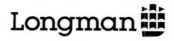

Contents

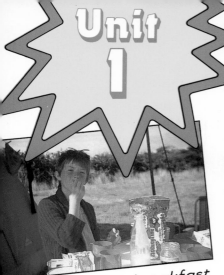

2. I was going for a swim when Dad took this one.

3. We saw some horses so Mum took this one.

We were having breakfast when I took this one.

4. My sisters went boating. This is the last one I took.

A. Question and answer

Choose the right answer to each question.

Questions
1. What was happening when the first photo was taken?
2. What was Sam doing when his father took the photo?
3. Did Sam's mother take a photo?
4. What was happening in the last photo?

Answers
He was going for a swim.
Sam's sisters were in a boat.
They were having breakfast.
Yes she did.

B. What were they doing?

Time	Sam	Diana	Tony
8.00	getting up	having breakfast	reading a comic
3.45	playing table tennis	swimming	playing football
9.15	going to bed	reading	watching television

Write sentences to say what they were doing at the times shown.

Begin like this

1. Diana was swimming at a quarter to four yesterday.

1. Diana (3.45)
2. Tony (9.15)
3. Sam (8.00)
4. Diana (9.15)
5. Tony (8.00)
6. Sam (3.45)

Unit 2

SUPERMARKET		
Mon.	9.00	– 6.00
Tues.	9.00	– 6.00
Wed.	9.00	– 7.30
Thurs.	9.00	– 6.00
Fri.	8.00	– 8.00
Sat.	8.00	– 5.00

POST OFFICE	
Monday–Friday	9.00 – 5.30
Saturday	9.00 – 12.00

BUTCHER	
Monday – Friday	8.30 – 4.30
Saturday	8.30 – 1.00

A. Let's get it clear

1. At what time does the supermarket open on Fridays?
   Begin like this

   > 1. The supermarket opens at 8.00 on Fridays.

2. At what time does the Post Office close on Tuesdays?
3. On what day does the supermarket close at half past seven?
4. Is the Post Office open at five o'clock on Mondays?
5. It's two o'clock on Saturday afternoon. Is the butcher's shop open?
6. How many of the places were open at quarter past five last Tuesday?
7. Will the supermarket be open at half past six next Thursday?
8. When Miss Brown went to the butcher's shop at five o'clock on Wednesday she found it shut. Where do you think she bought some meat?

B. When is it open?

> The butcher's shop is open from half past eight till half past four on weekdays, and from half past eight till one o'clock on Saturdays.

Write a similar sentence to tell someone when the Post Office is open.

 **Match them**

10.30	10.35	10.40	10.45	10.50	10.55
1	2	3	4	5	6

Match these times with the two ways of telling the time in words.
Begin like this

1. 10.30   *ten thirty or half past ten.*

ten forty	ten to eleven
ten fifty-five	five to eleven
ten thirty	half past ten
ten fifty	twenty-five to eleven
ten thirty-five	quarter to eleven
ten forty-five	twenty to eleven

 **The apostrophe**

the butcher's shop   the giant's huge foot

The apostrophe s ('s) shows that something belongs
to someone or something. The shop belongs to the
butcher, and the huge foot belongs to the giant.
   Look at the pictures on this page and on the opposite
page. Then make up a sentence about each of these:

1. the post lady's sack
2. the butcher's apron
3. the giant's clothes
4. the giant's face
5. the giant's size
6. the club's weight

What a monster

Imagine that the impossible happens. You come face
to face with a giant. Write a paragraph telling us
about the giant. Then write another paragraph about
what the giant does when you meet him.
You could begin like this

*It had just gone eleven by the Post Office
clock when the pavement suddenly began to
shake. The next moment I saw an enormous....*

Unit 3

Many years ago the birds all met to choose a king of the birds. 'A king should have beauty,' said the peacock displaying its beautiful tail.

'That's nonsense,' said the owl. 'Wisdom is what we want in a king.'

'I think we need someone who talks well to be our king,' remarked the parrot.

'No,' said the nightingale, 'the one we choose for king must be able to sing melodiously.'

'Not at all,' said the eagle fiercely, 'We must choose as king the bird who can fly the highest.'

As the eagle was so big and powerful, the other birds felt obliged to agree that this was the best way to choose the king. So they decided to have a test to see which bird could fly the highest.

At a signal, all the birds flew up into the sky. Each bird did its best, but soon the great eagle soared above them all. Higher and higher, and higher still rose the eagle, until it was exhausted with the effort.

'I have flown the highest,' cried the eagle.

'The test hasn't finished yet,' said the tiny wren that, unknown to the eagle, had been perched all this time on its great back.

Then the wren jumped off the eagle's back and flew a little higher still. In this way the wren became the King of the Birds.

 A. Let's get the words clear

Find the words in the fable that have these meanings:
Begin like this

> 1. *displaying*

1. showing off
2. in a pleasant tuneful way
3. very strong
4. forced
5. rose into the air
6. made very tired; worn out

 **Let's get the facts clear**

1. Why did all the birds meet?
   Begin like this

   > 1. The birds all met to choose a king of the birds.

2. The peacock thought they should choose the king according to the beauty of the bird.
   How did the owl think they should choose?
3. Which of the birds thought they should choose the king according to how well the bird could talk?
4. Why do you think the nightingale wanted to choose the king according to how well the bird could sing?
5. Whose way of choosing did the birds use?
6. Why did they choose this way?
7. How did the little wren manage to fly higher than the eagle?

wren

coot

reed warbler

 Dictation

Wrens build a dome-shaped nest with a very small opening.
They usually build it in a bank or at the root of
a tree. It is made of dry leaves or moss and then
lined with feathers and finer moss. Six to eight eggs
are laid. They are pale with reddish spots.
When the young wrens leave the nest, the hedges
seem full of them.

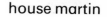

house martin

Now it is your turn

Choose any bird you like. Tell us about
its nest in a similar way.

Unit 4

bakery a building where bread is baked
brewery a building where beer is brewed
chef a person who is a trained cook
chemist's a shop where medicine is sold
chisel a tool for slicing off small
pieces of wood
choir a group of people singing together
hangar a building where aircraft are kept
harpoon a weapon used in hunting whales
or big fish
scissors an instrument for cutting paper,
cloth, etc.
sculptor a person who carves in stone
or wood
shipwright a person who builds or
repairs ships
shoal a large group of fish of the same kind

A. Nouns

Make five sentences by giving each beginning its right ending.

1. The noun chisel	is the name of a weapon.
2. The noun hangar	is the name of a shop.
3. The noun harpoon	is the name of a tool.
4. The noun chemist's	is the name of a group of people.
5. The noun choir	is the name of a building.

B. Proper nouns

Nouns are words that name things, people and ideas.
Notice that there are special names for places, things and people.
France is the special name of a country.   **Dr Brown** – a doctor
Birmingham – a city   **Waterloo Bridge** – a bridge   **Susan** – a girl
The Daily Mail – a newspaper

These are the special names of what proper nouns?

1. Spain   4. Thames   7. Mrs Mack
2. Paris   5. Henry VIII 8. Everest
3. Thomas 6. Asia   9. Captain Scott

city	country	officer
boy	river	mountain
king	woman	continent

6

C. Using the dictionary

1. What do sculptors do?
2. What can you buy at a chemist's?
3. What sort of group is a choir?
4. What is made in a brewery?
5. What is a weapon for hunting large fish called?

D. Alphabetical order

The words at the top of the opposite page are in alphabetical order.

The word brewery comes before chef. (Look at the first letters.)
The word bakery comes before brewery. (Look at the second letters.)
The word chisel comes before choir. (Look at the third letters.)
The word chef comes before chemist's. (Look at the fourth letters.)

Now put each of these lists in alphabetical order.

1		2	3	4
artist	acrobat	matron	Smith	wise
auctioneer	announcer	mason	Smart	white
barber	artist	librarian	Simms	watery
acrobat	athlete	mechanic	Smollet	warm
announcer	auctioneer	newsagent	Sinclair	wild
athlete	barber	jockey	Sissons	windy

E. Collections

We talk of a choir of singers and a shoal of fish. Make ten more phrases like this from the table

1. a flock of sheep
2. a bunch of

Collective nouns

Nouns that name collections are called collective nouns. Choir, flock, bunch, shoal are all collective nouns.

1.	a flock		flowers
2.	a bunch		fish
3.	a herd		sheep
4.	a clump		rare stamps
5.	a shoal	of	trees
6.	a collection		cows
7.	a litter		ships
8.	a fleet		puppies
9.	a flight		wolves
10.	a pack		aeroplanes

Unit 5

Invention	Date	Inventor	Nationality
Microscope	1590	Z. Jansen	Dutch
Cement (Portland)	1824	Joseph Aspdin	British
Sewing machine	1829	Bart Thimmonier	French
Dynamo	1831	Michael Faraday	British
Car (petrol-driven)	1885	Karl Benz	German
Jet engine	1939	Sir Frank Whittle	British
Nylon	1938	Wallace Carothers	American

 Let's get it clear

1. When was the sewing machine invented?
2. Who invented the jet engine?
3. What was the nationality of the man who invented the microscope?
4. The microscope was invented towards the end of the sixteenth century.
   In what century was the car invented?
5. Had the dynamo been invented when the first petrol-driven car appeared?
6. How many of these things had not been invented by the end of
   the nineteenth century?

Let's make some sentences

> *The microscope was invented by Z. Jansen in 1590.*

Make a sentence like this to say by whom each of the other things was invented.

 Nationality

Make a sentence to tell us what the nationality was of each inventor.
Begin like this

> *1. The inventor of the microscope was Dutch.*

 Adjectives with a capital letter

The jet engine was a British invention. Notice that the word British begins with a capital letter. It tells us about the invention and is therefore an adjective. It is formed from the proper noun Britain. Adjectives that are formed from proper nouns begin with a capital letter.

Proper noun	Adjective
Christ	Christian
France	French
Ireland	Irish
Jamaica	Jamaican
Paris	Parisian
Mars	Martian
Scotland	Scottish
Wales	Welsh

What proper nouns do these adjectives come from?
1. French
2. Welsh
3. British
4. Jamaican
5. Martian
6. Scottish
7. Irish
8. Christian
9. Parisian

 Punctuate it

Write this out with the proper capital letters and punctuation marks. Then turn to page 4 and correct your answer.

at a signal all the birds flew up into the sky each bird did its best but soon the great eagle soared above them all higher and higher and higher still rose the eagle until it was exhausted with the effort

 Let's find out

Try to find out more about one of the inventions. How was it invented? How good was the invention? How much has it changed since?

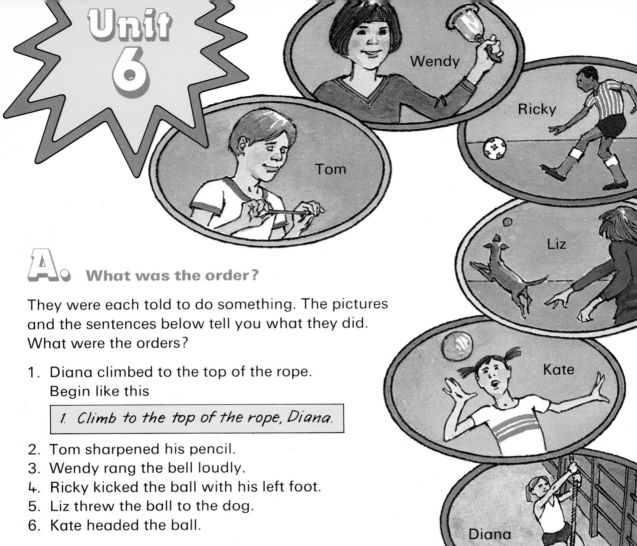

Unit 6

A. What was the order?

They were each told to do something. The pictures and the sentences below tell you what they did. What were the orders?

1. Diana climbed to the top of the rope.
   Begin like this

   > 1. Climb to the top of the rope, Diana.

2. Tom sharpened his pencil.
3. Wendy rang the bell loudly.
4. Ricky kicked the ball with his left foot.
5. Liz threw the ball to the dog.
6. Kate headed the ball.

B. Using verbs

Notice the words used to tell the children what to do:

climb   sharpen   ring   kick   throw   head

These doing or action words are called verbs.
Choose a verb to complete each of these sentences:

1. Detectives — crime.
2. Everyone — the performance loudly.
3. You — trees with an axe.
4. The sculptor — a horse out of stone.
5. Gagarin was the first man to — the Earth.
6. Mr Lee — his car to the garage last week.

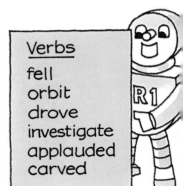

Verbs

fell
orbit
drove
investigate
applauded
carved

C. **Short sentences**

Make sentences by adding the best verb to each noun.

Begin like this

1. *Ships are launched.*

Nouns	Verbs
1. Ships	are felled.
2. Photos	are laid
3. Eggs	are caught.
4. Money	are launched.
5. Trees	are serviced
6. Fish	are blown up.
7. Tyres	are taken.
8. Jugs	is saved.
9. Cars	are educated.
10. Children	are filled.

 D. **More detail**

Lengthen the sentences you made in **C** by adding a phrase to say how or why.

Begin like this

1. *Ships are launched into the sea.*

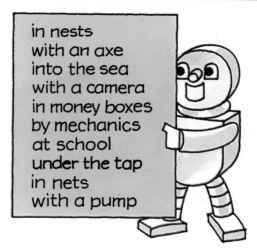

in nests
with an axe
into the sea
with a camera
in money boxes
by mechanics
at school
under the tap
in nets
with a pump

E. **A noun-verb alphabet**

a b c d e f g h i j k l m n o p q r s t u v w x y z

Nouns name persons, animals, things: **dancer, pig, door.**

Verbs tell us what they do: **jumps, grunted, are serviced.**

Make a sentence for each letter of the alphabet. The person, animal or thing (noun) does something, and the verb begins with the same letter. Use the lists on the right.

Nouns		Verbs	
cat	flags	drilled	zigzagged
idea	Vicky	kick	joked
monkey	zebra	plunged	x-rayed
rain	Xenia	arrived	questioned
officer	tigers	caught	ordered
ball	elephants	flap	bounced
dentist	wheel	showed	hovered
lady	astronaut	visited	lent
pirate	kangaroos	rattled	muddled
John	Nick	grow	wobbled
queen	youths	eat	interested
hawk	gardeners	undid	noticed
uncle	signpost	yelled	terrify

Lisa began like this

1. *The astronaut arrived late.*
2. *The ball bounced over the wall.*

11

Unit 7

KINDS OF SENTENCE

Statements Tom is not at school today. He switched off the light.	They give information. They state a fact, an idea.
Questions Is Kate going to the party? Have you brought your camera?	They ask for information. You ask a question then want an answer.
Commands Put up your hands. Don't forget to lock the door.	They give orders. They tell you to do or not to do something.
Exclamations What a delicious pudding! How well she plays!	They show your surprise. They exclaim.

 Let's get it clear

1. Which kind of sentence always ends with this punctuation mark?   ?
2. What is the punctuation mark called?
3. Which kind ends with this punctuation mark?   !
4. What is the punctuation mark called?
5. When do you ask a question?
6. With what kind of sentence are orders given?
7. When do you use statement sentences

 What are they?

What kind of sentence is it?
1. What is his brother's name?
2. Do up your shoe, Diana.
3. This book is called *Your English 4*.
4. What a stupid thing to do!
5. Where did you go yesterday?
6. How they keep teasing him!
7. Don't leave your clothes on the floor, John.
8. Is this the last one?

2. Ann 3. Derek 4. Vicky 5. Ali 6. Jane

1. Keith

C. Giving orders

What were the orders given to make them do these things?
Write command sentences. Tom began like this

> 1. *Close your left eye, Keith.*

D. What have they just done?

They have just done these things. Write six statement sentences
to state what they have done.

Begin like this

> 1. *Keith has just closed his left eye.*

E. Punctuate it

Here is an example of each kind of sentence.
Write it out with the proper capital letters and punctuation marks.

1. what is william's telephone number
2. what a beautiful view
3. the first real helicopter flew in 1939
4. switch off the cassette player for a moment jimmy

F. Let's make sentences

Make a sentence to fit each of these situations.

1. You want to know when the programme starts. (question)
2. You want to tell Mr Taylor that it is raining hard. (statement)
3. You exclaim that Julie plays the guitar very well. (exclamation)
4. You want to tell Peter to stop pulling the rope. (command)
5. You tell your friend what the capital of France is. (statement)
6. You want to stop someone from touching the kettle. (command)

In 1722 Jacob Roggeveen was sailing across the Pacific Ocean. He was sailing into an unknown sea. He was 3,800 kilometres west of the coast of South America. Very few ships had sailed so far west, and Jacob Roggeveen did not know what he might find there. He was looking for the Southland – a big country which many people in Europe believed lay somewhere in the Pacific Ocean.

On Easter Day one of the ships sighted land. It was only a small island, about 23 kilometres long and 12 wide, but Jacob Roggeveen hoped that the coast of the Southland might be close by. He didn't know that the sea stretched for thousands of kilometres to the west. There were small islands scattered across the ocean, but even the nearest of these was 2,000 kilometres away.

Because it was Easter Day, Jacob Roggeveen called the island he had found Easter Island. When he went ashore, he was astonished at what he found there. The people lived in huts, thatched with reeds. They had few clothes and only some stone tools. But everywhere on the island there were giant men, carved out of stone. Some of the stone giants were over 10 metres tall. They had round topknots of red stone on their heads.

Galapagos Islands

Pitcairn Islands

Easter Islands

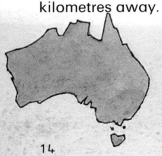

Let's get it clear

1. When was land sighted?
   Begin like this

   > 1. Land was sighted on Easter Day 1722.

2. Why did Jacob Roggeveen call the place Easter Island?
3. What do you think Southland really was?
4. What surprised Roggeveen so much about Easter Island?
5. Did Jacob Roggeveen live in the seventeenth or the eighteenth century?

 Pronouns

> Jacob Roggeveen called the island that Jacob Roggeveen had found Easter Island.

It sounds wrong when we repeat the noun (Jacob Roggeveen) in this way.
It is much better if we use **he** instead.

> Jacob Roggeveen called the island he had found Easter Island.

Little words like **he, you, I, we, they** – that are used instead of nouns –
are called pronouns.

Find three different pronouns in the extract opposite. Think what
the writer would have had to say if pronouns did not exist.

 Nouns/Pronouns

Rewrite these sentences, putting a noun
instead of each pronoun in **bold** type.

Nouns
Telescopes Pilots Susan
William   (A) tadpole

1. **They** bring ships into harbour.
2. **It** is a baby frog.
3. **He** plays in goal.
4. **She** is a nurse in the Middlesex Hospital.
5. **They** are used for seeing things at a distance.

 Punctuate it

Write out these sentences
with the proper capital
letters and punctuation
marks. Then turn to page 12
and correct your answers.

1. is kate going to the party
2. he switched off the light
3. how well she plays
4. don't forget to lock the door
5. what a delicious pudding

I'm Joe Sands from Leeds in Yorkshire, and this is my photo. I'm wearing a T-shirt, a pair of jeans and a jacket. I've got sneakers on, but you can't see my feet. The spaniel was a present on my eleventh birthday. In the six months he has been with me I have trained Patch completely, and he now goes everywhere with me.

My name is Pauline McIntyre and I live just north of Edinburgh. I'm just twelve and am wearing my riding clothes in the photo – a jacket, a sweater, a pair of jodphurs, boots and the obligatory hard-top hat. I'm holding my pony Silver Cloud. He's five years old and has already won a dozen or so rosettes at gymkhanas.

 Let's get it clear

1. Where does the girl with the pony live?
2. What breed of dog is Patch?
3. Why do you think that Pauline's clothes are warmer than Joe's?
4. How old is Joe?
5. Why do you think that a hard-top hat is obligatory for Pauline?
6. In what ways are Joe's clothes different from Pauline's?

B. What about you?

Pauline gave these details about herself.
Write a similar set of sentences about
yourself, making them true for you.

1. I live in a village north of Edinburgh.
2. My favourite sport is pony riding.
3. My pony is my pet, and I have a cat too.
4. At home I like video games best.
5. I read too, mostly pony stories.
6. I have lunch at school in the canteen.
7. My favourite school subject is PE.
8. I usually watch television for about
   an hour before going to bed, and I
   never miss the show jumping programmes.

C. Andy's routine

Write this out, putting words
for the pictures.

cereal
half past eight
jam
bus
wakes up
glass of milk
gets up
cup of tea
nine o'clock
toast
cleans his teeth
a quarter past seven

Most mornings Andy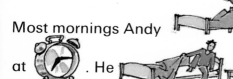

at . He

and then he has breakfast.

He usually has some

and then some with butter and .

Sometimes he drinks a with his breakfast, but more often

it is a . He always  before leaving for

school. He goes to school by . The bus comes

at about and school starts at .

The Arabian horse, which has been in existence for a long time, has been crossed with other breeds to produce very fast horses with great powers of endurance. Swiftest of all is the British Thoroughbred, which excels in bearing, shape, speed and jumping ability.

An adult male horse is called a stallion, and the female a mare. Young horses are known as foals, the male being a colt and the female a filly. Young foals are very curious about their surroundings and will investigate anything new by circling round to examine it from all angles, sniffing it as they do so.

Like most young animals, the foal is also very playful and will buck and run, often racing around with playmates of its own age.

Horses have a keen sense of smell, sight and hearing. They have a great awareness of movement too. Domestic horses recognise their keepers in the same way as they recognise each other – by sight, voice and smell.

Today, this magnificent creature is equally at home in the show jumping ring, in herding sheep and wild cattle in the outback of Australia or in competing in a great variety of sports; and it can look resplendent amid all the pageantry of military displays and ceremonial occasions. Yet it is still one of man's most faithful servants – a noble, intelligent animal that has befriended and served man for so many years.

A. Understanding the words

Find in the extract the words that mean:

1. a male horse
2. a female horse
3. a young male horse
4. a young female horse

5. tame; not wild
6. jump rapidly into the air
7. very splendid; gorgeous
8. made friends with

B. Understanding the matter

1. How do young foals try to find out about something new?
2. What do foals do when they are playful?
3. Which of the five senses do horses use in recognising their keepers?
4. What are four activities in which horses take part today?
5. Which type of horse is the fastest?

C. Say it another way

Give the same meaning by beginning with the words given.

1. We call an adult male horse a stallion.   An adult male horse . . .
2. We call a young female horse a filly.   A young female horse . . .
3. We call a female horse a mare.   A female . . .
4. People have crossed Arabian horses with other breeds.   Arabian horses . . .
5. Horses recognise their keepers by sight, voice and smell.   Their keepers . . .

D. Find out and write up

Horses have ways of communicating with one another. Sometimes these ways speak as clearly as words. The affection of mother and foal is always apparent from the closeness they keep to each other. Sniffing nose to nose is a common greeting. Two horses will often cement a friendship by nibbling, and so grooming each other's neck.
Find out how other animals communicate.

The badger digs its burrow in a wood. The tunnels may go as deep as five metres, with passages connecting special rooms for sleeping and others for nursing the young. The whole group of burrows is called a set.

   The badger keeps its home very clean and tidy. The sleeping rooms are lined with soft plants that the badger uses as bedding. The badger changes its bedding regularly, collecting fresh plants. It shuffles backwards towards the entrance of the burrow, holding the plants between its forelegs.

 A. **Two paragraphs**

This extract is written in two paragraphs.
Which heading best tells you what the first paragraph is all about?
Which best tells you what the second paragraph is all about?

The badger's tunnels
The depth of badger's tunnels
How the badger digs its home
The plants the badger collects
How the badger looks after its home
How badgers hold plants

B. Adding sentences

When we use sentences, we don't just string them together in any order. One follows another in a sensible order. You can see this by finding the sentence that naturally follows each of the numbered sentences below.

1. John wrote the name and address on the envelope.
2. The road was safe to cross now.
3. London is the capital of Britain.
4. Apes are the animals most like human beings.
5. I am very short, but my brother is very tall.

Choose from these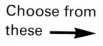

> Like us, they walk on two legs and have arms.
> Then he stuck on the stamps.
> People call us the long and short of it.
> The Lollipop Man waved us across.
> Though not the biggest in the world, it is a very big city.

C. Add another

To each of the pairs of sentences you wrote in **B** add another sentence chosen from this list:

Fifty years ago it was ranked as the largest of all.
We don't in the least mind their little joke.
The next moment he was on the way to the letter-box.
It was at the other side that we found the lost puppy.
Sometimes their behaviour is uncannily human.

D. A jumbled paragraph

Put the sentences in the best order to make a good paragraph.

Then they make their first visit outside.
Young badgers are born in their mother's set in early spring.
They stay near the entrance of the set to begin with.
After a week or two they grow bolder and move off
    to explore the wood nearby.
They do not go outside the set till they are about
    six weeks old.

Here comes number 6. He's leading the others by a few centimetres. His rivals are all bunched up just behind him. Let's have a closer look at him.

Look he's a very young man. He's running very smoothly and showing no sign of strain. Can the others overtake him? There is still a fair distance to the finishing tape and anything can happen yet.

A. Put him right

What a commentator!
He has got it all wrong.
Sort him out. Write down
what he should have said.

eight	sweating
many metres	straining
strung out	breasting
old	winner

B. Some howlers

Put these right with Robot's help.

1. We smell with our ears.
2. There are eight days in a week.
3. An annual event happens every month.
4. You consult a dictionary to find out where a country is.

year
seven
atlas
noses

C. Sort it out

The person	What he or she needs	to do what
1. A carpenter	a rod and line	to keep the money in
2. A fireman	a rolling pin	to guide the horse
3. An angler	a hammer	to make pastry
4. A jockey	a till	to put out the fire
5. A cook	reins	to drive in nails
6. A shopkeeper	a hose pipe	to catch the fish

Make a sentence to say what each person needs to do the job.
Begin like this

> *1. A carpenter needs a hammer to drive in nails.*

D. Now it's your turn

In the same way make a sentence to say what
each of these needs to do the job.

1. a hairdresser   3. a fisherman   5. a hunter
2. a farmer   4. a gardener   6. a sailor

E. Punctuate it

Write this out with
the proper capital
letters and punctuation
marks. Then turn to
page 18 and correct
your answer.

> horses have a keen sense of smell sight
> and hearing they have a great awareness
> of movement too domestic horses recognise
> their keepers in the same way as they
> recognise each other by sight voice and smell

F. What about you?

Add sentences to this to make
a paragraph about your mistake.

> *Like everyone, I sometimes make mistakes.*
> *For example, the other day....*

Did you know that when it hatches the young cuckoo pushes the other eggs out of the nest? To start with, the hen cuckoo takes an egg out of another bird's nest and then lays her own in its place. The other bird does not notice the cuckoo's egg when she returns to the nest. When the young cuckoo hatches, it wriggles under the other eggs one at a time and pushes them overboard. It then gets all the food!

Did you know that moles keep a larder? Moles live mainly on worms. They dig tunnels under the ground to find them. If at any time they find more than they need, they bite off their heads and store them in a 'larder'.
The decapitated worms grow new heads and are alive and ready to eat a few weeks later when the moles need them. The mole is an energetic creature and will eat its own weight in food every day!

Did you know that albatrosses fly round the world? They are the largest flying birds in the world and nest on islands near the Antarctic. They spend most of their lives circling the world, gliding always eastward on the west wind, until they come back again to the islands where they nest. The largest albatross has a wing span of three metres.

A. Let's get it clear

1. What is the unusual thing the albatross does?
2. What does the cuckoo do before laying an egg in another bird's nest?
3. How does the baby cuckoo make sure it has the nest to itself?
4. Why do moles need a lot of food?
5. Why do you think the mole bites the heads off the worms?
6. When an albatross flies round the world, where does it start
   its flight and where does it finish?

B. Let's make some sentences

Make six sentences by giving each beginning its
right ending.

1. Pictures are painted
2. Cars are serviced
3. Books are written
4. Racehorses are ridden
5. Dinners are prepared
6. Buildings are designed

by authors.
by jockeys.
by chefs.
by artists.
by architects.
by mechanics.

C. Say it another way

Rewrite the sentences saying what each person does.
Begin like this

| 1. Artists paint pictures. |

D. Punctuate it

Write this out with the
proper capital letters
and punctuation marks.
Then turn to page 22 and
correct your answer.

here comes number 6 he's leading the
others by a few centimetres his rivals
are all bunched up just behind him
let's have a closer look at him

E. Now it's your turn

Find out some unusual facts about something which you think will
interest others. Then write a paragraph about it to tell them.
Begin like this

| Did you know that...? |

You need

a long bread roll
some lettuce
some cooked chicken
an onion
a cucumber
two lollipop sticks
salt and pepper

Instructions

First wash your hands.
Take the long roll and cut it into two, longwise.
Hollow out each half by removing some
    of the soft bread.
Line the halves with crisp lettuce leaves.
Take the chicken meat off the bone
    and cut it up into small pieces.
Peel the onion and the cucumber, and cut
    those into small pieces too.
Mix them with the chicken meat.
Fill each half roll with the mixture.
Add salt and pepper to taste.
Thrust the lollipop sticks through leaves of
    lettuce and stick them into the top of
    the mixture to make sails.
You now have two delicious sandwich boats.

A. Order, please

Chris carried out the instructions and
made two sandwich boats.
In what order did he do these things?

He made the sails and stuck them in.
He lined the two halves with lettuce.
He mixed the chicken, onion and cucumber.
He ate one of the sandwich boats.
He cut the long roll in two.
He piled the mixture on top of the lettuce.
He hollowed out the halves of the roll.
He cut up the chicken and then the onion and cucumber.

B. What you did

Pretend that you made
the sandwich boats yourself.
Tell us what you did.

Begin like this

> First I washed my hands.
> I took the long roll....

C. Tell us how to do it

Someone from another country, who has never
made scrambled egg on toast, wants to know
how to make it. Give full instructions. Make
a list of what you need first. Then give step
by step instructions about what to do.

Begin like this

> Break the egg into a bowl and
> whip it with a fork, adding
> salt and pepper to taste.

D. Cooking or carpentry?

Which of these verbs
are most likely to be
used in cooking and
which in carpentry?
Make two equal sets.

sawed	grilled	glued
baked	screwed	seasoned
boiled	whipped	poached
fried	chiselled	drilled
nailed	steamed	planed
hammered	filed	tasted

27

 Six differences

One photo was taken a
little later than the other.
The camera was in the
same position, but six things
had changed.
Can you spot them?
Make sentences like this

> 1. In the first photo the dog is
>   running, but in the second
>   it is sitting down.

 Which words

Which words, then, would
you use when talking
about the first photo and
which when talking
about the second?
Make two equal sets.

C. What's the difference?

What is the difference between frogs and toads? As a rule, frogs have smooth skin while toads have warty skin.
In addition, frogs are usually more slender.
   Write two or three sentences to tell us what the difference is between these:
1. ponies and horses
2. bicycles and scooters
3. trucks and vans
4. oranges and tangerines
5. books and magazines

a toad

D. Adjectives

Half of these adjectives describe things pleasant to eat, and half describe things unpleasant to eat. Write them out as two sets.
Begin like this

pleasant	unpleasant
delicious	uneatable

Adjectives	
delicious	tender
uneatable	tough
tasty	juicy
stale	poisonous
fresh	disgusting

E. Easily or with difficulty?

Which of these verbs express actions done with difficulty and which express actions done more easily?
Make two equal sets.

Verbs	
plodded	dawdled
struggled	slipped
glided	strolled
laboured	toiled
rested	strained
strove	jogged

F. Two paragraphs

Build each of these into a complete paragraph by adding sentences. Be careful to keep to the one topic.
1. Horses have been put to good use. Over the years they have been more useful than any other animal.
2. The tractor has taken the place of horses on the modern farm. With its help the farmer can do most of the work without strain.

The weasel gave three gasps and fell back. Bevis looked at him a little while, and then put his foot on the spring and pressed it down and took the weasel out. He stroked down his fur where the trap had ruffled it, and rubbed the earth from his poor paws with which he had struggled to get free. Then, having chosen a spot close by the wood pile, where the ground was soft, to dig the hole, he put the weasel down. He pulled his limbs out straight, and so prepared him for the last ceremony. He then ran to the summerhouse, which was not far, and, having found the spade, came back with it to the wood pile. But the weasel was gone.

There was the trap; there was the place he had chosen – all the little twigs and leaves brushed away ready for digging – but no weasel. He was bewildered, when a robin perched on top of the wood pile, put his head on one side, and said softly and sadly, 'Bevis, Bevis, little Sir Bevis, what have you done?'

For the weasel was not dead, and was not even seriously injured; the trap was old, and the spring not very strong, and the teeth did not quite meet. The weasel was extremely thin, and so he escaped with a broken rib.

 A. **Let's get it clear**

1. How did Bevis get the weasel out of the trap?
2. How did the weasel's claws come to be covered with earth?
3. Why did Bevis dig the hole at the spot near the wood pile?
4. Why did he run to the summerhouse?
5. What had Bevis done to the ground where he was going to dig the hole?
6. Why was he bewildered when he returned to the wood pile?
7. What sort of trap was the weasel caught in?
8. The weasel was able to run off. Why hadn't it been seriously injured?

 B. **Compound words**

Each word needed to fill the first blank is a compound word.
That is, it is a word made up of two shorter words.

1. An — is a — which has arms.
2. A — is a — in which you can grow flowers.
3. — is a — which grows in the sea.
4. A — is a — that keeps out the rain.
5. — is — that is done at home.
6. A — is a — that is used in the summer only.

> seaweed
> homework
> summerhouse
> armchair
> flowerpot
> raincoat

 C. **Now it's your turn**

In the same way, make a sentence to say what each of these is:
1. a classroom
2. a teapot
3. a racehorse
4. moonlight
5. a doorstep
6. sunlight
7. a newspaper
8. a videotape
9. your birthday

D. **Imagine**

Imagine that you were the weasel. Tell us
what happened from the weasel's point of
view. Start at the moment the weasel went
near the trap and finish when it ran off.

August					
Sun.	–	6	13	20	27
Mon.	–	7	14	21	28
Tues.	1	8	15	22	29
Wed.	2	9	16	23	30
Thur.	3	10	17	24	31
Fri.	4	11	18	25	–
Sat.	5	12	19	26	–

My diary	
20th Aug.	Arrive Seatown Explore beach
21st Aug.	Picnic on beach
22nd Aug.	Visit fun fair
23rd Aug.	Motorboat trip along coast
24th Aug.	Hire canoe
25th Aug.	Play clock golf
26th Aug.	Visit zoo

 Let's get it clear

It is Saturday 19th August today. Tomorrow Emma starts her summer holiday at Seatown. She has got the first week all worked out. She has written in her diary what she is going to do each day.

1. What is Emma going to do when she reaches Seatown?
2. Is she going to visit the fun fair on Monday or Tuesday?
3. When is she going to visit the zoo?
4. What has she planned to do on 23rd August?
5. What is she going to do on Thursday?

 Looking back

Let's pretend that the first week of Emma's holiday is over.
It is now Sunday 27th August.

1. What did Emma do yesterday?
2. What did she do on 23rd August?
3. When did she go out in a canoe?
4. What did she do the day before yesterday?
5. What happened a week ago?

Let's pretend again

Let's pretend it is 16th August today.

1. Is it Tuesday or Wednesday today?
2. What was the date yesterday?
3. Was it 9th August a week ago?
4. What will the date be in a week's time?
5. What day will 31st August be?

 Join them

Make five sentences by adding the right ending to each beginning.

1. At the zoo Emma saw . . .
2. For pudding at the restaurant we had a choice of . . .
3. When she explored the beach, Emma found . . .
4. Coal, wood, charcoal, gas and oil . . .
5. Under the heading of ships she listed . . .

> Remember to separate the items with commas.

are all types of fuel.
a star fish, some winkles, two small crabs, lots of limpets and a cave.
tankers, trawlers, liners, cruisers and yachts.
lions, tigers, bears, elephants and giraffes.
fruit salad, trifle, cheesecake, jelly or ice cream.

 Shopping

Emma visited the newsagent's, the butcher's and the ironmonger's. These are the items she bought. Which did she buy at each shop? Begin like this

some nails	a magazine
a pork pie	a hammer
a newspaper	some liver
six screws	a trowel
some sausages	a leg of lamb
a comic	some envelopes

1. Emily bought a newspaper, ... at the newsagent's.

 Your holiday

What do you plan to do on your next summer holiday? Write a paragraph to tell us. If you have no plans, tell us what you would like to do most.

Unit 18

Sharp nose raised,
He centipedes by,
Three dogs long . . .
And half a dog high.

A round, smooth hull
For his tail to steer,
And two little squat legs
Bringing up the rear.

Clive Sansom

A. Choose the ending

1. The dog in the poem is . . .

> long and tall
> short and long
> neither tall nor long

2. He 'centipedes by' means that the dog . . .

> gallops past
> creeps by
> goes past like a centipede

3. The dog's little legs are . . .

> strong
> thick and short
> rather long

4. The hull is the body of a ship. The poet likens the body of the dog to a hull because it seems . . .

> to be steered by its tail
> so long
> so strong

5. The poet is describing . . .

> a greyhound
> a dachshund
> a spaniel

B. Rhymes

Find a rhyme for each of these words:

1. by
2. steer
3. fed
4. news
5. hair
6. fight
7. two
8. what
9. nose

Begin like this

> 1. by–high

toes	there
head	squat
high	you
rear	fuse
write	

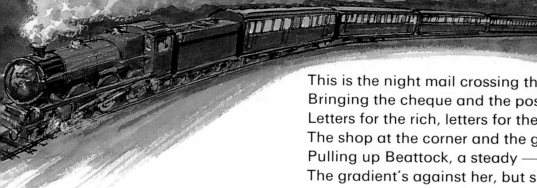

This is the night mail crossing the —,
Bringing the cheque and the postal —,
Letters for the rich, letters for the —,
The shop at the corner and the girl next —,
Pulling up Beattock, a steady —,
The gradient's against her, but she's on —,

C. The night mail train

This is the beginning of a famous poem by W. H. Auden about the night mail train from London to Scotland.

1. Copy out the six lines, putting in the missing words.
2. What is the 'border' that the train is crossing?
3. A gradient is a slope. What, then, is the meaning of 'the gradient's against her'?
4. What are the three kinds of things that the train is bringing to Scotland?
5. The train is on time in spite of something. What?

climb
door
poor
border
time
order

R1

D. Order, please

Here are the jumbled lines of a limerick.
Write them out in the proper order.

He was married, they say,
There once was a young fellow of Perth,
And he died when he quitted the earth.
On his wife's wedding day,
Who was born on the day of his birth.

E. Punctuate it

Write this out with the proper capital letters and punctuation marks. Then turn to page 24 and correct your answer.

the other bird does not notice the cuckoos egg when she returns to the nest when the young cuckoo hatches it wriggles under the other eggs one at a time and pushes them overboard it then gets all the food

It was growing dark underneath the lighthouse. The sea lapped quietly against the rocks and everything was still.

Every few minutes the beam from the lighthouse flashed out to sea and shone over the water.

Mandy looked up at the evening stars and then turned to her brother and said,

'Come on, Allen, it's getting late. We ought to go home soon.'

They had been fishing for two hours and they had only caught one fish. Once more Allen cast his line to sea. It wasn't long before he felt the rod jerk.

'I've got something,' he said. 'It's a big one from the feel of it.'

Mandy quickly reeled in her line and watched her brother. His face was shining with excitement as he struggled to reel in his catch. The rod bent until it looked as if it would break. Mandy leaned over the rails to get a better view, as up from the water came a dark shape, spinning on the end of the line.

But it was no fish that hung there dripping with water. It was a box bound with metal bands. Allen swung the box over the rocks. Then he and Mandy bent down to examine it. From the fastening in front of the box there came a chink of light.

'What is it?' Allen asked.

 Make your choice

Choose the best word and write out the complete sentence.

1. Mandy and Allen were fishing `by, near, below` the lighthouse.

2. The sea was very `rough, calm, noisy.`

3. Mandy said they ought to go home because it was getting `late, dark, wet.`

4. Allen thought he had caught a large `crab, box, fish.`

5. Allen had really caught a `rock, box, crab.`

 Joining words

> Tom lives in North Street. Kate lives there too.
> Tom likes drawing. Kate does not like it.

Notice how we can join the sentences with **and** or **but**:

> Tom lives in North Street, and Kate lives there too.
> Tom likes drawing, but Kate does not like it.

Make one sentence of each of these pairs by joining them with **and** or **but**.

Conjunctions
Words that join parts of the sentence are called conjunctions, such as but or and.

1. The sea lapped gently against the rocks. Everything was still.
2. We lit the fire. The sticks were too damp to burn.
3. We won the match. I don't think we will win the next one.
4. I watched television for a while. Then I went to bed.
5. The ball came towards Joseph. He put up his hand to catch it.
6. I like living in the country. John prefers living in the town.

 What was it?

What did the light come from? Did it have magic powers? What did they do with it? Tell us what you think happened.

Unit 20

Hill Farm
Pitfold
Exeter
 Devon EW3 1X
10th Aug. 1983

Dear Mum and Dad,
                    The coach ride was quite
enjoyable and the packed lunch was delicious!
Uncle, Aunt, Steve and Jane were all at Exeter
to meet me.

   That was two days ago. Since then I have
been a farmer! In spite of all the machines,
life on a farm is still very different from life
in a city street. I _am_ glad I came! Steve and
Jane have taken me everywhere with them. I
have already ridden a pony, worked a milking
machine, mounted a tractor and collected
dozens of eggs.

   Much too busy to say more at the moment.
Please write and tell me what is going on in our
street. Everyone here sends their best wishes.

                    Love from
                      Liz

P.S. Aunt Susan's cooking is fabulous!

Hill Farm
1 Pitfold
 Exeter
2 Devon EW3 1X
 10th Aug. 1983

3 Dear Mum and Dad,
                4 The coach ride was quite
enjoyable and the packed lunch was delicious!
Uncle, Aunt, Steve and Jane were all at Exeter
to meet me.
5 That was two days ago. Since then I have
been a farmer! In spite of all the machines,
life on a farm is still very different from life
in a city street. I _am_ glad I came! Steve and
Jane have taken me everywhere with them. I
have already ridden a pony, worked a milking
machine, mounted a tractor and collected
dozens of eggs.
   Much too busy to say more at the moment.
Please write and tell me what is going on in our
street. Everyone here sends their best wishes.

                6 Love from
                  Liz **7**

8 P.S. Aunt Susan's cooking is fabulous!

A. Setting out a letter

This is the skeleton or plan of the letter.
What is each numbered part?

the greeting
the signature
the second paragraph of the letter
the writer's address
the ending
postscript or tailpiece
the first paragraph of the letter
the date the letter was written

Begin like this | 1. The writer's address |

B. Let's get it clear

1. What was the name of the village Liz stayed in?
2. Who met her at the end of the coach journey?
3. What was the date when she arrived at Hill Farm?
4. What word did Liz use to show that her cousins had been specially kind to her?
5. How did she show that she had been very busy?

C. Join the parts

Join the parts of these sentences by putting in the right joining words or conjunctions.

Conjunctions

till
because
if
and
though

1. We need rubber boots — the field is very muddy.
2. They will cut the corn tomorrow — it is fine.
3. Let's stay in the barn — the rain has stopped.
4. We ate our lunch by the pond — enjoyed it very much.
5. Liz was not frightened — the bull came very near her.

D. Punctuate it

Write this out with the proper capital letters and punctuation marks. Then turn to page 36 and correct your answer.

but it was no fish that hung there dripping with water it was a box bound with metal bands allen swung the box over the rocks then he and mandy bent down to examine it from the fastening in front of the box there came a chink of light

E. Now it's your turn

Imagine that you have gone away on holiday on your own. Write a letter to your parents or a friend telling them how you are getting on. Or imagine you are Liz's mother. Write to Liz telling her all about what has been going on at home.

Unit 21

Leela

Andy

Colin

Ali

Diana

Emma

 A. **Who said it?**

Copy out the sentences, putting in the names of the speakers. Make sure you copy the punctuation exactly.

1. 'It's a delicious ice cream,' said —.
2. 'I'm going to have a swim,' said —.
3. 'Can I speak to Nick, please?' asked —.
4. 'How much does this one cost?' asked —.
5. 'These flowers are for you, Mum,' said —.
6. 'What a marvellous save!' exclaimed —.

B. **Question and answer**

Copy each question carefully and add the answer to it.

1. 'Have you any brothers, John?' asked the teacher.
2. 'Would you open the door for me, please, John?' said Liz.
3. 'Have you ever been to Cornwall, John?' asked Mrs Jones.
4. 'Why weren't you at school yesterday, John?' asked Miss Green.
5. 'What's Mr Day's telephone number, John?' asked Brenda.

'Yes, we went there for our holiday last year,' said John.
'I'm afraid I don't know it,' said John.
'Of course I will,' said John.
'No, I haven't any,' replied John.
'I had to go to the hospital for an examination,' he replied.

C. Say it another way

> 'Where have you put my brown shoes, Dad?' asked Chris.
> 'I'm going to play in the park, Dad,' said Chris.
> 'Would you mind lending me your calculator, Wendy?' asked Chris.
> 'It's great, this new video game!' exclaimed Chris.

Write down the sentence that has the same meaning as each of these:

1. Chris told his father that he was going to play in the park.
2. Chris asked Wendy if she would lend him her calculator.
3. Chris exclaimed that the new video game was great.
4. Chris asked his father where he had put his brown shoes.

D. Let's make the sentences

What were the words they spoke? Begin like this

> *'What is the capital of Australia, Colin?' I asked.*

1. You wanted to know the capital of Australia and asked Colin.
2. You told Sam you had left a sweet for him on the table.
3. You wanted to know if Cadiz was in Spain and asked Mr Day.
4. You wanted to know the time and asked Wayne.
5. You wanted to know how much the cassette cost and asked Sue.

E. Asking politely

Notice the polite way of asking someone to do something for you.

Suppose Pat wanted people to do the things listed below. Write out her requests as they would appear in a story book. Begin like this

> *1. 'Would you mind fetching me a chair, please, Liz?' said Pat.*

1. Pat wanted Liz to fetch her a chair.
2. She wanted Colin to lend her his torch.
3. She wanted her mother to tell her the time.
4. She wanted her father to move his chair back a little.
5. She wanted Joe to pass her the salt.

Would you mind opening the door for me please Tom?

41

Unit 22

 A. **Order, please**

Put these sentences in the proper order to tell the story of Grace Darling.

They successfully took off five of the crew.
Grace Darling, who was born in 1815, was the daughter of
  a lighthouse keeper.
Grace and her father speedily launched their boat.
One night as a storm raged violently, she saw a ship in distress.
Later, Grace and her father were awarded gold medals for
  their courageous act.
Then she bravely took an oar and helped her father row through
  the rough sea to the sinking ship.

42

B. How?

How did the storm rage? It raged violently.
How did they launch the boat? They launched it speedily.
How did Grace take the oar? She took it bravely.
How did they take off the crew? They took them off successfully.

> ## Adverbs
> Words that tell you how things are done are called adverbs.
> Violently, speedily, bravely, successfully are all adverbs.
> Most adverbs are formed from adjectives by adding –ly:
>   violent – violently;   brave – bravely

What adjectives are these adverbs formed from?

1. successfully
2. carefully
3. carelessly
4. gently
5. easily
6. timidly
7. angrily
8. hopefully

C. Let's make adverbs

Make an adverb from each of these adjectives:

1. merry
2. bold
3. quick
4. idle
5. angry
6. brave
7. easy
8. proud
9. steady
10. sensible
11. unhappy
12. capable

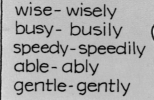

> ### Spelling adverbs
> slow – slowly
> wise – wisely
> busy – busily
> speedy – speedily
> able – ably
> gentle – gently

D. Sentence building

Make five sentences by giving each beginning its right ending.

1. Larks were singing
2. The peacock was strutting
3. We watched the bees flying
4. The tortoise crawled
5. I could see monkeys climbing

busily from flower to flower.
happily high above the corn.
agilely through the branches.
proudly across the lawn.
slowly towards the lettuce.

E. Now it's your turn

Make sentences to say what someone did:

1. gently
2. cruelly
3. boastfully
4. painfully
5. uselessly
6. guiltily

Tom began like this

> 1. The boy gently patted
>   the dog on its head.

43

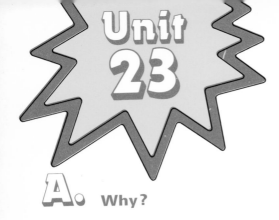

Unit 23

A. Why?

Make six sentences to say why they go there.

1. People often go to the Post Office
2. You usually go to a snack bar
3. We generally go to the library
4. People usually go to the airport
5. I went to the newsagent's shop

to borrow a book.
to buy a newspaper.
to catch a plane.
to buy stamps.
to have a light meal.

B. Let's do a word puzzle

Copy the puzzle onto paper. Then write down the words in this puzzle. Choose your words from the list.

Nouns	Adjectives	Verbs	Adverbs
minibus	careless	wobble	busily
players	smooth	anchored	nimbly
Tuesday	straight	advance	quickly

1. A small bus.
2. Without roughness.
3. In no way crooked.
4. The third day of the week.
5. To go forward.
6. In a busy way.
7. The people who play in a team.
8. In a nimble way.
9. Not taking any care.
10. Put down the anchor.
11. To move unsteadily from side to side.
12. At a fast pace.

C. Clothes

Where to wear them – on the head, the feet or the body? Make three sentences. Begin like this

> 1. We wear caps, helmets, hoods and berets on the head.

shoes	vests	jackets
caps	boots	berets
helmets	hoods	T-shirts
pullovers	sandals	slippers

D. They sound alike

beach the land at the edge of the sea
beech a tree
blew what the wind did
blue the colour of cloudless skies
fare money paid for a bus ride
fair light in complexion; blond
heard took in the sound of something
herd a collection of cattle
hole an opening; a hollow
whole all of it
meat the flesh of animals to eat
meet to come together

Choose the right words and write out the sentences.

1. We went down the beech, beach for a swim.

2. John ran down the path to meat, meet his friend.

3. Alex heard, herd a sudden crash and jumped up.

4. The cold wind blew, blue so hard it made his fingers blew, blue.

5. The fair, fare girl paid the conductor her fair, fare.

6. Can you eat the hole, whole slice, or shall I cut it in two?

E. Fancy dress

You have received this invitation. Say what you will go as and describe what you will wear.

> Dear....
>   I am having a fancy dress party at 6.30 on 15th August. I do hope you can come. Please let me know.
>   From Susan Ashby

Unit 24

A. Punctuate it

1. how difficult this is
2. the cake was hard stale tasteless mouldy and uneatable
3. have you ever been abroad john asked miss lake

B. One word for several

Rewrite each sentence using one word in place of the words in **bold**.

1. Miss Smith has just been to the **shop that sells medicine**.
2. Vicky was listening to a **group of people singing together** on television.
3. John's father is a **person who brings ships into harbour**.
4. We need a **tool for driving nails** for this job.
5. He bore the pain **in a brave way**.

C. Answer the questions

1. Are ladybirds insects or birds?
2. What is the opposite of heavy?
3. What do jockeys do?
4. Can dogs climb trees?
5. What were you doing at this time yesterday?
6. Do adjectives tell us what things are like?

D. Tell the story

kite
flying
string
high
reach
idea
drive
stand